RETIREMENT DOMINATION:

PLAY TO WIN WITH YOUR RETIREMENT

RETIREMENT DOMINATION:

PLAY TO WIN WITH YOUR RETIREMENT

BY TOM JACOBS

RETIREMENT DOMINATION: PLAY TO WIN WITH YOUR RETIREMENT

© 2020 TOM JACOBS

ISBN: 978-1-7325893-3-9

Printed in the United States of America
Year of First Printing: 2020

TABLE OF CONTENTS

DEDICATION

To my family and especially my wife Shelly for allowing me to be the person God designed me to be. It is rare for me to be home before 8:00 pm or for me to work less than seventy hours a week. Shelly's understanding and patience allows me to do what I love which is helping to protect my clients' money from market declines and avoiding crazy fees.

ACKNOWLEDGEMENTS

Thank you to Curtis James, the man that recruited me, coached me, and showed me a path to become one of the industry's top producers. Also thank you to Brett Kitchen, one of America's best marketers. Brett has helped me refine my message and share my ideas through print and radio marketing.

CHAPTER 1

FORGET THE NEST EGG, GET INCOME INSTEAD

(Get Your Money the Hell Out of There)

"AND WHETHER OR NOT YOU KNOW IT, RISK IS ALL AROUND YOU AS YOU SAVE FOR THE FUTURE."

Martin Ruby

B efore you start reading this book, I'd like you to go to the front cover right now and take a look at my author photo.

Did you do it? Good.

Folks, you just looked at one of the most blessed humans to walk planet Earth. What do I mean by that?

I'm talking about getting to have dinner every Sunday with my mom and dad.

As far back as I can remember, I've had the great blessing of eating dinner with my parents on Sundays. In fact, this Sunday you'll find me sitting down at the table enjoying a home-cooked family meal with my parents. In my opinion, that makes me one of the luckiest men to walk planet Earth. (Those of you who have lost your parents can appreciate how fortunate I am.)

Every Sunday we go through the exact same routine, I walk in and immediately kiss my mother on the cheek while she's cooking, then I get a cold beverage from the fridge and join my dad in front of the TV. This comforting family ritual has been the staple of my adult life — that is until something changed in 2008.

One Sunday, I walked into my parent's condo as usual. It was already late afternoon, and yet there were no familiar smells coming from the kitchen. Where my mother would normally be cooking at that hour, it was empty. Instead, she was sitting on the couch, seemingly absorbed in her thoughts, looking at some paperwork, and my father was nowhere to be found. I could immediately tell something wasn't right.

"What's wrong?" I asked her, over and over.

She just looked up at me and shook her head. "Nothing," she said.

My father came into the room, I looked over at him, but he only gave me a tight-lip smile and said the same thing. According to them, "nothing was wrong."

Neither of them were giving me a straight answer, so I decided to stop pressing the issue. They obviously weren't ready to talk. The next Sunday, I found a similar scene. My mother was preoccupied, and my father looked tense. Something was definitely wrong.

Again, I asked them what was wrong, and they brushed it off. As we sat down to dinner, I wondered if it was a health problem, or some other family crisis they were hiding — my mind was racing. This went on week after week, and with it my stress and worry only grew.

Finally, one Sunday I was sitting in the living room with my mother and out of the corner of my eye, I saw my dad go into the garage. I followed him, and found him waiting for me, sitting on the back end of his car, elbows on his knees, hands clasped. I thought, *Here it comes.*

He said, "Tommy, your mother and I can't tell you how much we appreciate your concern. We're overwhelmed, but I was hoping we'd never have this conversation with you. We've lost our nest egg, and we're scared."

Holy cow, I thought.

Even today, thinking back on this moment, all the hair on my neck raises up. There I was talking to my childhood hero, my best friend, my mentor — my dad. The man who had been so successful at everything he did in life was now telling me he was *scared*. I'd never heard those words come out of his mouth before.

As I dug deeper into the story, the details started coming out...

Both of my parents were big savers. They'd retired after working forty-two years with a nice sum of money saved in a 401K account, enough for a comfortable retirement. When the market tanked in 2008, I wasn't too worried about them, as I knew they had their nest egg. But three months into the recession, my parents started losing hundreds of thousands of dollars. Unsure what to do, they kept it to themselves. During this time, I had been going to their house, every single Sunday and I had no idea what was going on. By the time my dad finally told me the truth that day in the garage, they'd already lost half of their savings.

This was devastating news to me.

My mom and dad had been robbed of their retirement, and it was all because they had been listening to bad advice. Understand, my parents are YOU. They're not irresponsible, or frivolous people. They don't wear Rolex watches or drive Bentleys; their biggest priority during their working years was saving up for retirement, and putting my brother and I through college. They did both those things quite successfully, and still wound up losing nearly everything, because we weren't able to catch it in time.

> "THERE ARE MANY AMERICANS OUT THERE, JUST LIKE MY PARENTS, WHO ARE STRUGGLING TO HANG ONTO THEIR MONEY. IT HAS GOTTEN EXCEEDINGLY DIFFICULT TO NAVIGATE RETIREMENT PLANNING IN OUR COUNTRY OVER THE LAST FEW DECADES."

If this story sounds familiar to you, it's because it's common. There are many Americans out there, just like my parents, who are struggling to hang onto their money. It has gotten exceedingly difficult to navigate retirement planning in our country over the last few decades.

And this is why I'm writing this book.

Let's face it, the traditional retirement path is broken. In the not so distant past, we had three key components to our retirement planning: our pensions, Social Security, and our savings, which was most likely a 401K. Today, pensions have all but disappeared. The share of U.S. workers who are covered by a traditional employer-sponsored pension plan has declined dramatically over the past few decades. According to some sources, even public sector jobs — once the bastion of the traditional employer pensions — are seeing shifts in coverage, especially for newly hired employees. Social Security is another questionable factor. As you know, all social welfare programs are subject to fluctuations in regulations, governance, and of course, the burden is ultimately on the American taxpayers.

So, this leaves only one strategy left, which is completely in your control: your savings.

Younger people obviously have more time to plan and save for retirement, and older people don't. This is why as we get older, and closer to retirement, we must reduce our exposure to market crashes — because there's simply less time to recover — and why it's so important you protect yourself, and your money, from these types of events.

Each time we experience a recession, it takes roughly six to eight years for our economy to recover. Fundamentally, we have less time to recover from such setbacks when we're older. To compound this, each market correction is worse than the previous. For instance, in 2000, the market showed a forty-nine percent decline, and in the recession in 2008, it was a decline of fifty-one percent. What will the next one look like? Nobody knows, but if history repeats itself, it will be fifty-one percent, at the very least.

That means if I want to retire and I'm sixty-two years old, and I lose half my money in a market correction, I have two options: I have to work longer, or retire with less money.

Does either one of those options sound ideal? No.

I'd like to help as many people avoid that scenario as I can. That's why I made it my mission to develop a bulletproof retirement strategy over the last decade, and I have been using it to safely guide my clients' money into safe financial vehicles, where they are guaranteed an income for life, that will only increase as they get older.

How did I come up with this winning strategy?

Well, it started during the 2008 recession. While my parents were experiencing their loss, I was going through my own financial downturn. In fact, it was the worst I'd ever experienced.

Prior to 2008, I owned a successful mortgage broker-age company for twenty years. With all the proceeds from my thriving business, I would reinvest in real estate, and over time I had created a nice little portfolio I nicknamed "52 front doors," a mix of multi-family units and rentals. My wife was also a real estate broker at the time, and she was heavily invested in the properties as well. In a nutshell, ALL our income at the time was related to real estate, making us 100 percent tied to the market.

When we woke up in March 2008 to read in the morning newspapers that Bear Stearns had collapsed, we knew we were in for a ride. As the market tanked, and financial institutions floundered, our property values went with them. Tenants were losing their jobs left and right, banks were closing, and people stopped paying their bills. Suddenly, I owed more mortgage debt than what my "52 front doors" were worth.

To make matters worse, we'd just purchased 100 acres of land that we were getting ready to develop. When I bought that land, I had signed a purchase agreement to flip it the next day, and that fell apart, too. Then my wife's business tanked. It was a comedy of errors. By the end of the year, much to my shame, we found ourselves in debt to the tune of $4 million dollars. I was in my early forties, and this was the lowest point in my life.

Falling flat on my face financially was the catalyst I needed to right the ship and get back on track. We needed a fresh start, so we moved from Michigan to Florida and got our real estate business up and running again. After a few months we were making a living, but not out of the water yet. During this time, the humiliation and stress of being financially stretched, not knowing how I would pay my bills, with two young girls that I was desperately trying to be a good mentor to, was unbearable. But all this awfulness turned around the day I decided to become a financial planner.

There was a huge need in the market for financial advisors, because soon I realized it wasn't just my mom and dad, but *every* Baby Boomer was struggling with their retirement. I set out to learn as much as I could, but after a few months of this, I realized I was moving too slowly. We weren't recovering fast enough. I intuitively knew I was missing the right tools. I thought, *There has to be a better way.*

I searched high and low for a financial product that was built for retirement. Within a few months, I discovered fixed indexed annuities and it totally changed the game for me. Since then, I've not only had the opportunity to help more people, I'm also proud to say my family has fully financially recovered.

> "THE FIRST THING I TELL MY CLIENTS WHEN THEY WALK INTO MY OFFICE IS, "YOU NEED TO GET YOUR MONEY THE HELL OUT OF THAT 401K."

I've been on all sides of this roller coaster — struggling, successful, flat broke — now I'm back on top, doing better than ever before. Over the last decade, I've helped hundreds of families safeguard their savings and create guaranteed income with my play-to-win retirement strategy. My general philosophy is this: I seek conservative growth and aggressive income. We want to park the money safely, without fees, but when it's time to start spending that money, it should be guaranteed for life, and only growing bigger. And the first thing I tell my clients when they walk into my office is, "You need to get your money the hell out of that 401K."

Here's why ... the story of my mom and dad.

My mom and dad had it all mapped out, but because they believed the advice of their broker, they left the entire nest egg in their 401K, and lost half of it. During the time of their lives that they were planning on spending their hard earned money and enjoying their retirement, they had to go into defense mode because the market was tanking. Now that they have the money back, it's totally pointless.

I like to use the casino analogy. If I handed you $10,000 right now, and we jumped in the car and drove over to the casino, it would be safe to say that the longer we stayed there, the less likely we are to leave with our money. That's why casinos are so big and beautiful, because the house always wins. Their priority is keeping you at the table, playing. The second you get up from the blackjack table they stop making money.

Similar to a casino, keeping you invested in the market is your broker's job. If your account is going up, he's making money. If it's going down, he's still making money. But if you stop investing, and take your money out, he stops making money. That's why the standard advice coming from brokers is to keep your money in financial vehicles that are tied to the stock market.

The reality is, the longer we leave our money in a 401K, the less likely we'll have it when we need it—and the only way to keep it all, is to get it the hell out of there!

Your broker isn't lying, he's just telling you what he believes based on his background, but at the end of the day, it's not his money. He's not sending your kids to Disney World or paying your nursing home bills — nobody on this planet cares as much about your retirement money as you do, except maybe your children.

So, who should be calling the shots when it comes to where you should be saving your retirement? You, obviously.

I want you to stop blindly listening to the garbage coming out of Wall Street. Morgan Stanley, Goldman Sachs, JP Morgan — these firms will never tell you the truth, because if they did, they would lose money. You've heard their message for so long and from so many different people that it's become the truth. Wouldn't you like to know if they've been lying to you sooner than later?

If you're anything like me, the answer is sooner.

If I could rewind time and go back and tell my parents all of this before 2008, I would, in a heartbeat. Unfortunately, nobody has invented a time machine yet. So, until that day, I'm helping to educate as many people as I can. I don't want what happened to my family, to happen to yours.

So, if you're ready for the truth, then keep reading. In the following chapters, I'll be telling you how money really works.

CHAPTER 2

The Biggest Lies Wall Street Ever Told

"I am more concerned with the return of my money than I am with the return on my money."

Roy Rogers

O ver my lifetime, I have followed some good financial advice and some terrible financial advice and suffered for it. Most of this bad advice came out of Wall Street, and it cost my family dearly. What do I mean? Let's take a closer look, specifically at what happened to my parents before their retirement crisis.

Late in 2007, my parents were just entering their retirement and began to roll their retirement accounts into IRAs. They met with their financial advisors at very reputable national name brand brokerage companies. Under their advisement, my parents invested their money very conservatively in mutual funds. Now, this wasn't bitcoin, or marijuana stocks, or anything risky. This was pretty conservative stuff, and yet, in a matter of eight months, my folks lost almost half of their retirement nest egg.

Why did this happen? Because financial advisors give the same advice to everyone, regardless of their situation. What they tell you is what they tell all their clients — keep your money in the stock market.

What they should have said is, "You guys have done a great job saving up your money. You've worked hard, you've built up this incredible wealth, now it's time for you to enjoy it."

Ideally, my parents should have taken those gains out of the market before the crash, so they could enjoy their retirement. Instead, the advisors wanted to continue to play with the money. They didn't warn my parents to take their nest egg out of the market and they successfully lost half of it. The retirement that my mom and dad worked forty-two years for, and diligently saved for, went down the drain.

Our entire lives, we've been communicated to and given misinformation from Wall Street. We've heard these lies so many times, and from so many sources, they've now become the truth. The wolves of Wall Street often come to us disguised as sheep. They say things like, "mutual funds aren't risky because they're diversified," or "you can invest in mutual funds, and forget about them until you need the money," or "mutual funds are long term and suitable for retirement."

And when the market drops and the inevitable happens to people like my parents, Wall Street shrugs its shoulders and says, "Hey, everybody loses money sometimes!"

It doesn't have to be this way. We can't predict the future, and we can't control the market — but we can control where our money is. We have no idea what will happen tomorrow in the stock market, nor do we know what it will look like the day we retire, or six years from now. A world leader might roll out of bed tomorrow and send a tweet and the market is down 1,000 points. You don't have to put your money in the market where it's exposed to loss, just because that's what 'everybody does,' or because an advisor told you to, or because Uncle Joe down the road does.

So, in this chapter I'm going to expose some of the biggest lies Wall Street has ever told; lies that have led to many bad decisions being made in the financial world. You may be surprised at how familiar you are with some of these common misconceptions.

Everybody pays fees.

I like to call this the 'Fee versus FREE' concept. Most people are under the impression that if you have a brokerage account, paying fees is customary; it's normal for you to pay an asset advisory fee, or an asset management fee, or an administration fee. The reality is that paying fees is **not** normal, and not everyone pays them. In fact, I'd say it's 100 percent optional. You never have to pay fees, not one penny, not ever. You just simply need to know where you can invest your money for free, where it is not subject to fees.

Let's say tomorrow morning I wake up and decide I'm going to open up the best checking account that I can possibly find in West Michigan. So I walk into Bank of America, or PNC Bank, or Sun Trust Bank, and set up the best checking account that I can find with all of the bells and whistles: free checks, online banking — the whole nine yards. But there's one catch — there's a $15 a month fee.

If I walk out of that bank and go over to the credit union on the other side of the street, and I set up that same checking account with all the bells and whistles, the credit union is free. There's no fees.

Well, which of those two accounts would be better for me? Obviously, the free one.

Think about it, these days you can't go to the local grocery store and back without driving by a new credit union. Credit unions aren't a new concept, they've been around for a long, long time, but it's only recently that the American consumer has begun to recognize that it's simply a better deal. Every day, millions of dollars leave our banks and go into credit unions. It's just that simple.

Now, if I asked you to consider doing the same thing with your 401K or your IRA, would you be interested? If we could take those same dollars and put them in a spot where there were no fees, all things being equal, I bet you would do it.

> "The point I'm making is that no matter what the financial industry tells you, paying fees is not normal. It's optional."

There is a famous quote from Jack Bogle, the American investor and founder of Vanguard Group, "[...] we investors as a group not only don't get what we pay for, we get precisely what we don't pay for." Bogle maintained that if you put your money in an account where you're getting a five to seven percent return on your money but paying multiple provider fees, over thirty or forty years you will end up making more money for the brokerage account than you did for yourself. These small fees may seem insignificant until you understand, through the power of compound interest, how they affect your account balance over time. Bogle was so "fee adverse" he insisted on lowering his own firm's (Vanguard Group) fees, and the compounded gains from investing the difference saved his shareholders $559 billion in forty years.

The point I'm making is that no matter what the financial industry tells you, paying fees is not normal. It's optional.

And if you continue paying fees, you'll only be letting others ultimately rob you of your gains.

It's normal to lose money sometimes.

This is one of Wall Street's favorite lies, "Hey! It's normal to lose money sometimes."

Not true!

This simply isn't the truth. Not everybody loses money, because not everybody has money in the market. Some people have their money in checking, savings, money markets, and CDs. If the market tanks, they're fine. I've personally met farmers who bury their money in coffee cans in the family farm. It may not be earning any interest, because that money is sitting in a can earning zero rate of return, but they don't lose a single penny when the market drops.

The only way they could lose that principal is if they forget where they buried the can.

Not everyone has their money in the market. If you do, then your fortune will go up and down. But if you don't play with that financial vehicle, there's no downs. So, to blindly say "that's just the way it is" is patently untrue.

Why does Wall Street tell this story? Because they only profit when you have money in your account. You have to understand the deep incentives at play here. There is no incentive for them to tell you to take your money out of the market. They need you to continue paying fees, and they need you to stay in the game — and they will say whatever it takes to get you to do that.

The dirty little secret is that fund managers rarely beat their benchmarks year after year. According to Marketwatch, one out of twenty actively managed domestic mutual funds beat the index. Something like eighty-seven percent of professional money managers cannot beat the S and P. By having somebody actively manage your money, you're actively having them lose you money.

So, when they say "everybody loses money sometimes" what they mean is that you will definitely lose money if you continue to allow them to manage your money.

Anybody who has played the stock market knows in their gut that the market cannot continue to go up forever. At some point it will tank. Everybody has a different risk tolerance. Some people enjoy taking big risks, losing money, and paying fees (I'm not one of them). The question is, when that happens, how much of your hard earned retirement savings do you want to have in there?

I don't know how much you're willing to lose, and how many fees you want to pay, but if I were you, tomorrow morning at nine o'clock sharp, I'd be pulling my money out of the market. Every damn penny.

Diversify your portfolio.

We've all heard this one: the key to keeping our money safe is having a diversified portfolio.

We're told our whole lives to diversify, diversify, diversify. In other words, don't put your eggs in one basket. And because we've been told our whole lives not to put all our eggs in one basket, we don't. We put our money into 401Ks, and IRAs, and in bank accounts, and in a variety of different mutual funds, etc. Our portfolio is diversified, and as a result, some of the positions we've invested in are going to do well, but some of them aren't.

Now we've got a scenario where the winners are offsetting the losers, and then we have the privilege of paying fees on every single dollar that's being invested in a rising market. The average mutual fund investor in the United States gets approximately one third of the return. So if the market goes up ten percent next year, the average investor doesn't get a ten percent return, they get much closer to three percent.

Why are we playing a game where the winners are off-setting the losers? We're paying fees the entire time, and the net return at the end of the day is about a third of what we would have gotten otherwise.

I don't know who popularized this investment strategy, but diversification is not the key to keeping your money safe, the key to keeping your money safe is putting it in a safe spot. According to Wall Street, people shouldn't put all their eggs in one basket, and I would say to that — find a *great* basket and put your eggs into it!

Every dollar you refuse to pay in fees to an active manager is a dollar of return that you've earned, not the manager. As Jack Bogle said, you get what you *don't* pay for.

Now that we've dispelled some of these myths and misconceptions, let's talk about the most common retirement vehicles Americans are using today to save for retirement — company retirement accounts, brokerage accounts, banks, and annuities — and the question is whether or not you think these are serving you well?

CHAPTER 3

FOUR COMMON RETIREMENT VEHICLES

"INVEST IN THE FUTURE BECAUSE
THAT IS WHERE YOU ARE GOING TO
SPEND THE REST OF YOUR LIFE."

Habeeb Akande

When my grandpa passed away, his wife Marleen came to me totally distraught. She had no idea where their retirement savings was, or the estate plan, or the tax returns, or the passports, etc. She was completely in the dark. My grandpa had always managed their affairs — he was the quarterback. Marlene on the other hand knew nothing, and when her husband passed away, it created a shithouse mess.

Now, when I meet with clients, I tell them, "One of you is the quarterback — you know where the money is, why the money is in that account, and it's your job to manage things. But both spouses need to be on the same page."

By the time you're done reading this book, I want you to have a general understanding of what you're doing and why, even if you aren't the 'quarterback.' The goal is to keep it simple, so that if the quarterback is the first to go, then the other partner isn't left with a mess on their hands. In order to do that, we'll need to start with the basics, nuts and bolts of retirement planning: your savings.

There are four main vehicles where people tend to put their retirement savings: banks and credit unions; brokerage accounts; company retirement plans; and annuities. We're going to examine the pros and cons of each one, so you can get a better understanding of the vehicle most suited to your retirement plan, and why.

Bank or Credit Union

The number one spot where people save their money is in a bank or credit union. As I mentioned in the last chapter, I certainly advocate having money in the bank or even better, in a credit union. When you have money in the bank, it's safe, and if it's in a Federally chartered bank, then you've got the added protection of FDIC insurance up to $250,000 dollars per account. But most importantly, that money is liquid, and we can touch it and play with it, or take it out and put it back in, anytime we want. It's absolutely critical to have your money in a place where you can access it at any time without asking anybody's permission. This is your emergency fund.

The bad news is that we're just simply not getting returns on those dollars.

There's a bit of a false sense of security when our money is in the bank. We think, "Oh my gosh my money is in the bank and it's safe, I can go visit it anytime, and take it out. It's 100 percent liquid." And we get all warm and fuzzy thinking about it. Unfortunately, like most people, we aren't thinking about the future.

> "THE FACT IS THAT THE NUMBER ONE THING THAT WE'RE GOING TO SPEND OUR MONEY ON BETWEEN TONIGHT AND THE END OF OUR LIFETIME IS HEALTHCARE COSTS, AND CLEARLY HEALTHCARE COSTS ARE RISING."

The fact is that the number one thing that we're going to spend our money on between tonight and the end of our lifetime is healthcare costs, and clearly healthcare costs are rising. Healthcare is the fastest rising cost sector in the U.S., going from five percent of the economy in 1960 to 17.9 percent in 2016, and getting more and more expensive at the rate of six percent every single year. According to Warren Buffet, healthcare costs are swallowing the economy like a "hungry tapeworm."

Sure, you've got the whole nest egg in the bank, it's safe and it's liquid, but it's not growing. Every year that money is depreciating in value as inflation rises, and bank fees eat away at the total. Chances are you're going to need that money down the road to pay for something that's only getting more and more expensive by the day. In other words, mathematically speaking, you're going backward at warp speed.

Retirement will likely come with some costs, such as healthcare, a nursing home, long term care, copays, deductibles, or even cancer surgery. Without a doubt, you're going to need that money. This is why it's extremely important to keep your money somewhere safe — but also growing.

Brokerage Account

The second most common place for retirement savings is in a brokerage account. I would suspect that many of you reading this book have a brokerage account with Edward Jones or Raymond James, or one of the other top brokers in the country. At the end of the day, there's only one reason why you have even $1 in a brokerage account, and the reason is because you're trying to grow it.

When you're trying to increase your wealth, the more risk you're willing to take, the more upside potential you have. In fact, there is absolutely no limit on how much you can make when your money is in a brokerage account, but there's also no limit on how much you can lose.

The second problem is that you are likely paying fees, not on some of the money, but on every single penny that you have invested. Then there's what I call 'management stress.' Most people don't realize that they're under this type of stress. These are the sleepless nights you spend wondering — do I allocate into that? Should I buy this? Or wait until after the first of the year?

That's called management stress. So, if you're ok with all of the downsides, the risk, and the hassle, then a brokerage account might work for your retirement plan. But, personally, I like to sleep at night.

Company Retirement Plan

The third most common place for retirement savings is your company retirement plan. This might be called a 401K, or it might be called a 403B, or it might be called a TSA, depending on where you work.

Let me just say right now, I love company retirement plans. I am a huge proponent of company held retirement plans, but only for one reason — and the reason I think company plans are so excellent is because of company matching.

Generally speaking, company retirement plans are great because it's a systemized, automatic way for people to save money over time. In my experience, most people, if they got their entire paycheck every other week, would just spend it. But because the 401K is in the way, a little bit of your money automatically gets put aside for your retirement, pay period after pay period, month after month. This gives you the opportunity to grow and build your wealth over time. But, in my opinion, it's even better when your employer agrees to match your contribution and puts some of their money in along with yours.

If your company offers to match your deposit, I would encourage you to contribute to your employer plan up to what they are matching, but not one penny more. If your employer offers you a 401K, but they don't match, then I wouldn't contribute a single penny. And the reason is: taxes.

In my experience, most people simply are not thinking about it that deeply. We are told (by Wall Street) to contribute as much as we possibly can into our 401K, because at retirement, we're likely going to be in a lower tax bracket. Well, that's a big fat lie.

> "THE TRUTH IS, MOST PEOPLE WHEN THEY RETIRE, WANT TO MAINTAIN THE SAME LIFESTYLE THEY HAD WHILE THEY WERE WORKING. AND THAT TAKES MONEY."

The truth is, most people when they retire, want to maintain the same lifestyle they had while they were working. And that takes money. If all your money is in your company sponsored retirement plan, the minute you pull the money out of there, the IRS will come for their share. And if you're taking money out to maintain the current lifestyle you have, you're not going to see a reduction in your taxes. They could even be more.

So, the bottom line is that 401Ks are great because of company matching, but if there is no match, then there are better places where you can put your retirement savings and still have the ability to take it out without having to pay taxes.

Annuities

The fourth financial vehicle for retirement savings is annuities. There are all kinds of annuities available, some of them are absolutely wonderful, terrific products, and some of them are absolutely horrendous, terrible products. Not all annuities are the same.

The most common annuity in the marketplace today, owned by more Americans than any other type of annuity, is called a variable annuity. According to the financial dictionary definitions, a variable annuity is an insurance product designed to allow you to accumulate retirement savings. You allocate the premiums you pay among the various separate account funds offered in your annuity contract — hence, variable.

There are some disadvantages, and according to Investopedia, "variable annuities are riskier than fixed annuities, as there is no assurance of returns being generated, if there is a withdrawal, then any capital gains are taxed as ordinary income, withdrawals made prior to the age of 59.5 may be subject to a ten percent tax penalty, and the fees can be quite hefty."

During my seminars, I always tell a story about a client of mine that had a variable annuity and was paying $28,000 a year in fees — and she had only had it for five years! By the time I met her, she'd already paid over a hundred thousand in fees, and there was nothing I could do to change that. This client, like many other people I've met, didn't understand how their variable annuity worked. In fact, not one single time in my life have I met a client that could tell me how their variable annuity actually worked. Most of the time, people tell me what they *think* is happening with their fees, and 100 percent of the time they are wrong.

While variable annuities are best avoided because of the high fees, there are other types of annuities that are available today where your money isn't at risk, you won't be subjected to crazy fee structures, and they can provide some really awesome benefits. In general, these types of annuities — called fixed index annuities — are a wildly popular place for people to save retirement dollars.

The point I'm trying to make here is that not all annuities are the same. There are great ones and there are terrible ones; there are some that charge money management fees and some that don't (we always recommend the ones that don't); and you need a financial advisor that thoroughly understands the ins and outs of all the different types available.

As a side note, if you own a variable annuity and suspect you're getting gouged by fees, there may be ways to get out of it. That being said, if you bought the annuity last Thursday, there isn't much anyone can do to get you out of it, because there are all sorts of nasty surrender penalties and fees. But if you've owned it for a while, there's a reasonably good chance you might be able to get your money out of it. And if you can get it out of that variable annuity, guess what? We're suggesting you should put it in a spot where you'll never lose it, you will pay zero money management fees on it, and there's less likelihood you'll be creating what I call a "tax time bomb" that is set to go off the second you start taking money out of the account.

What's a tax time bomb, you ask?

I'm glad you asked. It's exactly what it sounds like —
it's what happens when we ignore taxes, and it's such
a pervasive problem in our retirement planning world
today, I've devoted the entire next chapter to make
sure you avoid creating one.

CHAPTER 4

TAX TIME BOMB

"THE UNINFORMED TAXPAYER WILL PAY MUCH
MORE IN TAXES THAN THE INFORMED TAXPAYER."

Marty Ruby

After a live dinner event in Michigan a couple of years ago, one gentleman checked 'yes' on the response sheet and scheduled an appointment at my office the following day. When he walked in and shook my hand, I wasn't expecting the man standing in front of me. Larry was an ominous figure, seven feet tall with tattoos on every inch of his body and a pony tail down to his butt. He was the type of guy that if you saw him in a dark alley, you'd turn and run the other way! Turns out, he was the nicest dude in the world.

He said, "Hey, Tom, I enjoyed the talk last night, I'm getting ready to retire next month — in exactly thirty days. I have three questions for you. One, I've got a pension, and I need to determine whether to take the lump sum, or take the single payments, or a spousal continuation? Two, what about social security? Do I turn it on now or wait until I'm sixty-six? How do we do that? And three, I work for the phone company and I've got a massive 401K that I've been saving money in for forty-two years.

"Here, I put together a spreadsheet," he said.

First, I was thrilled he took the time to do this spreadsheet. We pulled it up on his computer and looked it over, and he indicated when he wanted to withdraw the money and how much. As I scanned the document, my heart sank. Nowhere on there did he account for taxes.

I said, "Larry, thanks for doing this — but where are the taxes?"

Larry sat there and looked at me like I had three heads. "Taxes?"

I continued, "All this money you've saved, this is not all yours."

He turned ghostly white.

The main problem is that Larry's situation is typical of many Americans, they aren't adjusting their retirement plan for taxes. Most are saving in tax deferred accounts like 401Ks, creating a massive tax situation that's set to explode the second they retire. In other words, Larry was sitting on "tax time bomb."

I told him, "The IRS has a lien on the money in your 401K, so part of it isn't yours. The second you withdraw the money you have to pay the IRS."

In Larry's case, he was in the thirty-three percent tax bracket, and so I had to break the bad news to him that he's going to retire next month with thirty-three percent less money, or, he has the option to work longer to recoup that tax "bite" coming out of his account. Both of those options are horrendous.

I truly felt bad for him. Like many Americans, Larry had gotten some bad advice.

From the second we enter the workforce, we are told to save as much as we can in our 401K and keep pounding away at it year after year. But that was a lie. They want you to believe when you retire, you'll drop down into a lower tax bracket, and it won't be that big of a deal. The truth is, when you retire, you're actually going to want the same lifestyle if not better than the one you enjoyed while you were working. You're going to want to enjoy your retirement, have fun, play golf, and travel — and that takes money!

The second you take the money out of your retirement plan, it's considered income and you'll pay taxes on it, at whatever bracket you're in. Some of you idealists might be thinking, well, what if taxes go down? If you look at history, it's pretty easy to predict that our taxes will go the way they've always gone — up.

Taxes

Will Rogers once said, "The difference between death and taxes is death doesn't get worse every time Congress meets."

In America, our taxes change every time we elect a new president. They also change with the needs of the nation, inflation, national debt, wars, and with various tax regulations and policies.

You may think that taxes have always been part of our history, but it hasn't always been this way. Actually, much of America's early history was tax free. However, the government had to figure out some way to collect revenue, so in the beginning, they put tariffs and duties on various items such as liquor, tobacco, and sugar, mimicking the types of taxes that had been collected under British rule.

Having just escaped the taxes of Britain, this didn't sit well with early Americans. Cue the Whiskey Rebellion in 1794, where a group of farmers, angry about the new taxes on liquor, burned down the tax collectors' houses, and tarred and feathered the tax men, forcing them to flee. Congress intervened with the military to suppress the rebellion. Unfortunately, the government wouldn't be dissuaded from implementing federal taxes forever. In the 1790s, a property tax was introduced to finance an expensive war with France. By the early 1800s, the U.S. government had added new taxes to finance the War of 1812 against the English, including higher duty fees and excise taxes.

All of these taxes, however, were minor compared to the taxes America was forced to collect to finance the most expensive war to date: the U.S. Civil War. Occurring during the industrial boom, this war carried with it costs in equipment, weaponry, machinery, and manpower. The American people paid for this with their taxes. By 1861, a few months into the war, and falling into massive debt, Congress passed the Revenue Act of 1861, which implemented income taxes on all incomes over $800. Eventually this Revenue Act was repealed, but nevertheless, the precedent had been set for what we know today as our modern U.S. tax system.

From this point forward, the government proceeded to extract revenue from the income of its citizens. Franklin Roosevelt's New Deal led to an increase of taxes that had citizens in the highest tax bracket paying a seventy-six percent tax rate. Taxes continued increasing all throughout the Great Depression, and America entered WWII. By 1940, American citizens making $500 or more income paid a twenty-three percent income tax, while the wealthiest were paying an outrageous ninety-four percent marginal tax rate.

Over the next three decades, the fifties, sixties, and seventies, the top federal income tax rate never dipped below seventy percent. The highest recorded tax rate during this time was over eighty percent. During the sixties and seventies, inflation grew government deficits, and taxes were indexed for inflation, which detracted from the value of people's incomes. This continued until the Economic Recovery Tax Act of 1981 cut the highest tax rates from seventy percent to fifty percent. In 1986, the Tax Reform Act, expanded the tax base, but dropped the rate down to twenty-eight percent. Policy makers claimed they would never raise it above twenty-eight percent again, but their promise only lasted three years before it was broken.

In response, Nixon lowered taxes with a series of Tax Acts during the 1980s and all individual tax brackets were lowered and continued to be reduced throughout the 1980s. During the 1990s, taxes once again began to rise, and the top rate jumped to 39.6 percent. Fluctuating slightly in the early 2000s, the tax rate stabilized around thirty-five percent until 2012, when the American Taxpayer Relief Act increased this rate back up to 39.6 percent, and the Affordable Care Act added an additional 3.8 percent on top of this, making the maximum federal income tax rate of 43.4 percent.

"Judging by the current state of affairs, our growing national debt, inflation, increasing government spending on social welfare programs, and the U.S.'s tendency to get involved in foreign wars frequently — taxes are going up, and you should plan for it, accordingly."

When Trump entered the White House, he rolled out a much anticipated tax reform plan in 2017 which would lower the highest income tax rate to thirty-seven percent in 2018, but he kept the additional 3.8 percent, making the top federal income tax rate 40.8 percent.

This short history lesson is important because it shows you how the tax law is always changing, and where we are currently at in the cycle of increasing and decreasing tax rates. You must pay close attention to these changes because they affect *your* bottom line. Judging by the current state of affairs, our growing national debt, inflation, increasing government spending on social welfare programs, and the U.S.'s tendency to get involved in foreign wars frequently — taxes are going up, and you should plan for it, accordingly.

Right now, taxes are "on sale."

Thanks to President Trump, tax brackets have been temporarily reduced. His tax reform plan is set to sunset in 2025, and who knows how high taxes will go next time. That is why I encourage people to take advantage of this situation while they can. This is a great time to convert any taxable retirement accounts you may have to non-taxable accounts. If you do that one thing before 2025, you'll get double the benefit because when you go to withdraw that money down the road, you won't be paying taxes on the gains from the growth.

In other words, I want you to address the tax situation in your retirement plan. Do it now, and don't wait. The last thing I want you to face at the time of retirement is a tax time bomb.

Some of you might be thinking, Tom, what if I've already created a tax time bomb?

This is more common than you think. When I talk at live dinners and ask the folks in the room, "Where are you saving your money?" More than half the people say — in their company retirement account, TSA, 401B, or 401K. I see three to seven families every day in my office, six days a week, and most of these people have their savings tucked away in their company 401K plan, and by the time we've crunched the numbers they don't want to keep their money in there.

Most people wait until their sixties to start thinking about retirement. The problem is you've been saving your nest egg in a tax deferred time bomb, and now you've only got two to four years before retirement. It's not too late, but before you retire and set off the bomb, you have to defuse that bomb!

It's essential that you put a tax plan in place now — don't save all your money in tax deferred accounts like 401Ks — there are other places to store money that won't create a tax time bomb waiting to explode when you withdraw the money. For instance, cash value life insurance, and Roth IRAs are two examples of products that allow you to pull the money out without paying taxes. But if you're going to keep the money in your 401K, then you have to account for taxes, and plan accordingly.

Even Larry, who was only thirty days away from his retirement, was able to salvage his retirement. Today, Larry is one of our best clients. I was able to figure out his pension and Social Security strategy, and we used an advanced strategy to transfer his money from the 401K into an annuity, and then into a tax-free cash value life insurance policy, and now most of his income is 100 percent tax free. Larry has a plan, and more importantly, he can never outlive his money. He's living a stress free retirement, and now he's able to do more comprehensive planning. The last time I saw him, he'd bought himself a new Ford F150 Raptor!

The bottom line is that a lot of people are sitting on a tax time bomb, unaware of how severe it is. My message to you is that even if you've waited until the last minute, and you're getting close to retirement, it's still not too late to defuse that bomb. But the time is now, not tomorrow. Redefine your strategy today and start converting some of the taxable money to non-taxable money, and you, too, can have peace of mind in retirement.

CHAPTER 5

The Poor Rich Man

(No Peace of Mind in Retirement)

"Financial freedom is freedom from fear."

Robert T. Kiyosaki

How can you be rich and poor at the same time? It might seem like a contradiction, but there are people out there who I would describe as poor rich men. My good friend Todd is one of them.

Last year, in July I turned fifty and my wife took me on a surprise fishing trip. Long story short, we ended up in Manitoba, Canada, fly fishing on the beautiful pristine Canadian lakes. I absolutely love to fish, so I had the time of my life.

Shortly after arriving home from this marvelous trip, my wife turned to me, and said, "Let's do it again, that was so fun.

"But next time we go, let's go with friends," she added.

She didn't have to ask me twice, I said, "Shelly, that sounds great!"

The next morning, I eagerly called Todd, and said, "Hey, you know that trip that Shelly and I went on and can't stop talking about? Well, guess what, we're going to do it again! And we'd love for you to join us."

And without hesitation, Todd said, "Geez, Tom, that sounds great ... but I'm going to have to pass."

Why? Because no fish is worth $3,500 dollars.

Todd is retired with plenty of money in the bank, two homes that are totally paid off, and zero debt. Plus, he's collecting Social Security, a pension, and rental income. The man has a bulletproof retirement plan, but even still, he's worried that he might run out of money. For instance, he's afraid to pay for internet service, so he doesn't have Wi-Fi in his home. He doesn't want to pay for trash service, so he takes it to the dump himself. Todd is so afraid of running out of money that he won't even enjoy the money he's got!

It boggles my mind.

Todd was seventy-eight years old and 100 percent debt free, and he still didn't feel comfortable going on a once in a lifetime fishing trip with friends. How many more shots will he get at something like this? The answer is none.

Like many other Americans, Todd is living day to day. Of course he knows he's got all this money, and yet he's living like he's poor. In the back of his mind, he's thinking, "Oh my gosh, what if there's a medical event? Oh my gosh, I might run out of money. I'd better not take that trip. I'd better not spend that money."

> "Not having a plan is a plan. It's just a bad one."

He's living in fear, and the reason he's living in fear is because he doesn't have a written plan!

Most people's idea of retirement planning is getting their statements in the mail every quarter, taking a very cursory look, and sticking it in a drawer somewhere. And the next quarter their statement comes again, they glance at it, and stick it in the drawer. If this is your retirement plan — you're setting yourself up for absolute disaster.

Not having a plan is a plan. It's just a bad one. It's a plan that will never enable you to have peace of mind in retirement.

Unfortunately, I wasn't able to convince Todd to put a written plan in place. He's a very good friend, but I didn't push it with him. Sometimes you have to just leave it alone. At the end of the day, we certainly missed him on the fishing trip.

If you're reading this thinking — that's me! I'm like Todd! My question to you is: What's the value of having money in your retirement account if you don't get to spend it? Nothing. So, create a plan.

Life is too short to be rich and live poor. We aren't guaranteed all the opportunities in the world. Create a solid plan today, so you can enjoy all of life's moments, without worry.

One Less Duck

One beautiful spring evening about an hour before sunset, my dad and I began slowly motoring out to a great little fishing spot on the lake to see what we could catch. As we were gliding along, we saw a few ducks about fifteen feet ahead, floating on the surface of the water. Suddenly, one of the ducks disappeared. My father and I looked at each other in shock. A monster pike had grabbed it, and with one swift motion — Bam! One less duck in the world.

The point of this story is, you never know when you will be the duck.

The number one concern of people between age fifty to eighty who are approaching retirement is running out of money! So many people are afraid of running out of money in retirement that they're spending less as a result, even if they have plenty of it, and in doing so, they're compromising the quality of life they would have if they were able to freely spend their money.

In other words, they're both rich, and poor.

What they really should be worrying about is not getting to enjoy the fruits of their labor before it's too late. We aren't guaranteed a certain amount of days on this planet; at any moment our time might be up. That's why I want you to spend your money sooner rather than later — when you're healthy, mobile, and able to enjoy life's experiences to the fullest.

Putting a plan in place so you never run out of income while you're alive allows you to relax and have fun. Because when you're ninety years old, in a nursing home, drooling on yourself, it won't matter how much is in your Raymond James or Charles Schwab account.

Let me give you an example.

Just this morning I met with a client who saved a little under one million dollars in retirement assets and is retiring very soon. When he first walked in, he looked very unsure about his retirement plan.

After crunching some numbers, I said to him, "Hey, if we just took half this million dollars, and we had no growth on it at all, and we just burned it and spent it down over the next ten years, that's still $50,000 a year."

I continued. "If we take the $50 grand, plus your $24,000 a year in Social Security, you've got $74,000 a year guaranteed for the next ten years. Do you think you could live on that?"

His face brightened up immediately.

That's just the worst case scenario. He's probably not going to blow through half a million dollars, but it's always good to know that even if he did, he'd still be all right. Next, what we did is create a bulletproof retirement plan, in writing, so he is completely certain that he will never run out of money. Then, we took a portion of his assets and put them in a fixed index annuity, and we'll use that account to create guaranteed income that's going to last the rest of his life. That account will be tax deferred, growing, and accumulating over the next ten years. So, even if he decides to spend down the other half a million bucks over the next ten years, the annuity money is still there, and that income is now guaranteed to be paid to him for the rest of his lifetime, and it can only get bigger.

It's just easy math. Now this client is 100 percent bulletproof. He doesn't have to think about his retirement, or worry about spending too much, because he's got plenty of money that's never going away. So if North Korea drops a nuclear bomb this afternoon, or if a politician tweets something outrageously stupid this afternoon, it doesn't matter. Even if the market crashes, it doesn't matter. This guy is all set, simply because he took the time to visit with me, and we put together a plan for him. Now he's off having fun.

> "The people that win with their money are proactive, and the people who are reactive, lose."

Again, it just comes down to doing some proactive planning. The people that win with their money are proactive, and the people who are reactive, lose.

Reactive vs. Proactive

Imagine that your money is in the stock market, and you're on your app, watching it go down, down, down. It's losing points by the second, and your portfolio is shrinking right before your eyes. Just think about it intuitively. What do you want to do? Do you want to pull that money out of there? Yes!

At some point you're going to look at that decreasing number and say, "I can't take it anymore."

Then you'll do something reactive — you'll take the money out.

Of course, as soon as you yank that money out of there, next month the market starts going up...

You see where I'm going with this. The client I used as an example, the one who is proactively managing his retirement account, proactively planning, and has an income plan and tax plan — well, he doesn't have to react to market conditions because he's already built out his plan. He's out having fun with the grandkids.

I use this analogy a lot when I'm trying to work with clients who are heavily invested in the stock market. Let's pretend that you are the head coach of the Michigan State basketball team. Your guys are playing in the National Championships this year against Duke, and the game is over. You just beat Duke 72-68. Now, let's say the official referee of the game walks over to you and says, "Hey, Coach, would you like to go to overtime?"

You'd scratch your head, and think — overtime? "What are you talking about? We just won!"

Here's the point I'm trying to make: you've already won in your retirement. If you never earn another dollar, but you've planned proactively, and have plenty of growing assets and savings, you can enjoy a great retirement. However, if you keep playing the game and the market makes a thirty percent correction, that's a whole other story.

In other words, quit while you're ahead.

So, if you're reading this and you have your retirement savings in a brokerage account, my question to you is: Why are you still messing around in the stock market? You've already won!

Stop playing around and get that money out of there today.

Your broker isn't going to tell you to take your money out of the market. When the market is down, they're going to say, "Hey, it's just a paper loss, don't worry about it." Now you've got to wait for the market to recover. Another thing your broker likely won't tell you is that we've experienced the longest bull run in the history of the world market today. It's at an all-time gain, with all-time highs. And that's not a "paper gain" it's real money.

Listen, if you keep your money at risk when you've already won, the odds of you losing it are very high. The market is going to go down, because there's only one direction to go from here. And eventually you'll freak out and pull your money out. So, you might as well get out while you're ahead.

The reason I'm putting so much stress on why you shouldn't put your nest egg in the stock market is because it makes planning extremely difficult. In the next chapter, we'll be talking about the bread and butter of retirement planning: income. In order to do accurate income planning we need you in a proactive position, not a reactive one. Keep reading because we'll be taking a look at income, and what your retirement will look like if you start planning early.

CHAPTER 6

Make a Bulletproof Income Plan

"You wouldn't get in a car and drive around aimlessly, hoping to arrive at a pleasant destination. So why would you consider doing this with your retirement?"

Koos Kruger

When a new client signs on with us, I give them a detailed summary of their retirement plan. It's a binder containing several different sections, and once I've handed it to them, I ask them to turn to the first page where their money is. This is not a thirty-two-page statement, it's just a one-page summary that shows them where their money is today, how much money is in their account, and how much the total is with the bonuses.

The other day, I gave my client Sally her binder. She sat quietly while I went through the booklet with her and showed her the deliverables, page by page.

I said, "Look, here's your Social Security tab where we've done a social security analysis. We've really looked at the best way for you to claim your income. Here is our income distribution tab ... this is basically the income plan we're going with, and across the top we're listing all of the buckets that are available to withdraw money from."

I pointed to the margins, and said, "Then along the side it shows when we're taking money from each of these accounts. And our goal is to create a plan for you where you have multiple checks coming in every month."

Like most of my clients, Sally was wondering what her retirement would look like. She asked, "Okay, what happens each month?"

I said, "Well, on any given day during the month, Sally, you will go to the mailbox and grab your Social Security check and while you're there you'll grab your pension check, and also you'll grab a check out of each one of these three fixed indexed annuities that I just showed you."

This client has five checks, and they're going to come in every single month as long as she's alive. Not only that, three of those checks can only get bigger and they are guaranteed to never go down.

The point I'm trying to make is this particular client has absolutely no fear that she's ever going to run out of money. What's even better is that it didn't take all of her money to create this excellent, enormous ongoing guaranteed income stream.

So I'm going to advise her to spend every single penny because next month when she goes back to the mailbox, she's going to have five checks waiting for her!

I am suggesting to her that she begins spending some of her assets today, right now, while she's young, she's active, she's mobile, she's healthy, and she has the time to travel and enjoy this. But if she didn't have this plan in place, she wouldn't be able to spend those assets, because that's not how she's wired — she's wired just like the rest of us (including you) — without a bulletproof plan, we're conservative people, and we spend less.

I don't want you to compromise the quality of your retirement by not spending your money. Like this client, I want you to have a bulletproof plan that allows you to freely spend your money and enjoy it while you're able to do so because tomorrow is not guaranteed. That's why I'm telling you to start income planning as early as possible, so your bulletproof plan is waiting for you when you're ready to retire.

Let's go through the first few steps of creating your own bulletproof income plan.

Put Your Money in a Safe Place

In Chapter 4, I told you the story of my client Larry (with the tattoos and ponytail) who came to me right before retirement and discovered he hadn't accounted for taxes, creating a tax time bomb that was set to go off the moment he withdrew his money from his 401K. Had Larry come to one of my seminars fifteen years ago, instead of fifteen days before he was ready to retire, he would have retired with a bulletproof tax plan, taken advantage of the current tax law, and saved hundreds of thousands of dollars in taxes.

Instead, I had to do what I call "retirement crisis planning" for Larry. We simply didn't have enough time for anything else, with him retiring in less than thirty days. As you remember, I gave him two horrendous options, he could either take significantly less money, or he could work longer to recoup the money he'd be losing in taxes.

All right. So which option did he take? Did he go ahead and retire in a month or did he keep working longer?

Well, he ended up retiring from the phone company he'd been working at for forty-two years. He took about sixty days off and then he went and got a part time job to supplement his income, and we deferred his social security a little bit longer. Now, this wasn't so terrible because Larry was still pretty young and active, and he was happy to make a career change to working on Harley's, which is his passion.

> "IN SHORT, THE NUMBER ONE, FIRST PRIORITY OF RETIREMENT PLANNING IS HAVING YOUR MONEY IN A SAFE PLACE, WHERE YOU'RE NOT GOING TO LOSE IT."

Then we started moving that money from his 401K into an annuity, and finally, we transferred it over into a cash value life insurance policy where his money would be in a tax-favored position, and accessible to him when he needs it. Then we created a Social Security plan so Larry would know exactly how he was going to claim and maximize his income.

In short, the number one, first priority of retirement planning is having your money in a **safe place**, where you're not going to lose it. That's number one. If you have your money in the stock market and the market corrects forty percent, your plans just went up in flames. So, that's why it's the most important thing, and often the first step we take.

Once we get the money in a safe spot, now the question is: how do we use these dollars to create an income plan? And that plan will address several different key areas: Social Security, taxes, and distribution. We need to understand where we will be taking the money from, and when.

Plan for Taxes

One of the biggest components of a bulletproof retirement plan is tax planning. Taxes take such a bite out of your income, if you haven't done a good job preparing for that "bite," you could wind up with a tax time bomb that's waiting to explode in your retirement account.

The most common mistake I see people make is that they don't start early enough. Most don't start thinking of retirement income until they're in their late fifties or early sixties, whereas if they had a tax plan in their thirties or forties, they could have easily avoided creating that massive overpayment.

I've said this in earlier chapters, but it deserves repeating: you need a tax plan.

One of the best examples of this is a client of mine named Dan. He didn't necessarily come to me early enough to prevent a tax time bomb, but we were able to defuse it pretty easily. We converted his traditional IRA into a cash value Indexed Universal Life insurance policy, and during the conversion process, we parked his money in an annuity.

Dan had around $1 million in his IRA, we rolled this into a fixed index annuity, with no taxes, no penalties or fees, and he even got a nice upfront bonus. After letting this money sit there for a year, he started taking advantage of the ten percent free withdrawals, taking out $100,000 per year, paying $25,000 in taxes, and converting the remaining $75,000 into payments for the premium of his IUL over a ten-year period. Now the money is growing tax free in his IUL, and Dan has the ability to take his money out at any time without paying any more taxes on it, along the way.

In addition to this, he's got a huge death benefit that can be used for long term care should that need arise, or if something were to happen to him. He has a bulletproof, self-completing retirement plan, that upon his death will provide benefits to his family, tax free, if he's able to complete the plan, which is obviously the goal.

All of this came about because he simply moved his money from a taxable bucket, to a non-taxable bucket. He had a tax plan.

Social Security and Distribution

Social Security planning is the piece of the income plan that deals with our claiming strategy for Social Security benefits, and the sequence of returns, such as what accounts we are grabbing money from, and whether we dip into the taxable or non-taxable accounts first.

This is the last stage of the bulletproof retirement plan, and by now you should have a pretty good idea of what your retirement will look like. The only thing left to do now is plan where you want to take the grandkids on vacation, and which golf course to sign up at!

This is the point, folks, if you don't have a plan, then you're living in angst and fear. (Remember my friend Todd.) I cannot tell you how many clients I see that come into my office looking for retirement planning advice that don't have an inkling about any of these things. Many of them have done a good job of saving up their money, but they have no plan. Our goal is to have our clients enter retirement with confidence; confidence is created when you have a plan.

"MY QUESTION TO YOU IS, IF YOU KNEW FOR A FACT THAT YOU COULD RETIRE AND NEVER RUN OUT OF MONEY, AND HAD MULTIPLE SOURCES OF INCOME COMING IN EVERY SINGLE MONTH FOR THE REST OF YOUR LIFE — WOULD THIS CONVINCE YOU TO PUT TOGETHER A PLAN?"

What happens if they don't put together a plan? Once they retire, all of the sudden they'll put a death grip on their retirement assets because they're so scared they might run out of money. They can't be sure if they have enough money to retire on, whether or not Social Security will cover enough of their living expenses, and exactly how much taxes they'll need to pay. They're terrified. In the back of their brain they're worried about expenses, and as a result they'll be compromising the quality of their retirement.

My question to you is, if you knew for a fact that you could retire and never run out of money, and had multiple sources of income coming in every single month for the rest of your life — would this convince you to put together a plan?

The bottom line is if you don't have a plan in place, it's impossible for you to trick your brain into thinking it's okay to spend money and enjoy your retirement. But if you know for certain, and your brain recognizes that — hey, it's impossible for me to ever run out of money! Suddenly, you can allow yourself to enjoy a stress free retirement.

Repeat after me: In order for me to have peace of mind, I need to have a plan.

Now that that's understood, let's talk about the different types of advisors and retirement planners out there in the financial industry, and why I use what's called the "Mother Standard."

CHAPTER 7

THE "MOTHER STANDARD"

"WHEN PEOPLE ASK ME IF I'M A FIDUCIARY, I SAY, "ABSOLUTELY NOT!"

Tom Jacobs

The other day a client walked into my office and said, "I've heard this word fiduciary on TV — are you a fiduciary?"

"Absolutely not," I said.

In fact, I have something that's even better than being a fiduciary. I use the "Mother Standard," and in my opinion, not only is it comparable, it's even more important to me. The "Mother Standard" means, I'm going to give you the same advice I'd give to my mom. If I wouldn't sell something to my own mother, I'd never recommend it to my clients.

It's all about doing what's right.

Everyone is hung up on this term 'fiduciary,' which is defined as someone acting in the best interest of others. They're under the impression that if you're not a fiduciary, you're not looking out for the best interests of your clients, but that's 100 percent a misconception.

Let me let you in on a little secret ... acting in good faith isn't exclusive to fiduciaries.

Those of us who operate in the insurance business have separate guidelines called "suitability" we adhere to, meaning that not only agents have certain standards they must follow, but the carrier that we send the applications to also has to review it and make sure that it's a suitable sale. There are inherent checks built into the system that keeps us from taking advantage. Regardless of whether I'm a fiduciary or not, everything I do has to make sense for the client.

So, fiduciary is a popular term that I've heard a lot of people throw around lately, with little understanding of what it actually means. Thanks to marketing and advertising telling people they shouldn't work with someone unless they're a fiduciary, many are going to assume working with a fiduciary is the gold standard. They're hearing: "Why work with an insurance agent or an advisor, when you can work with a fiduciary?" When there is no reason for me to become a fiduciary, because I don't believe in selling products that aren't in my client's best interest.

Wall Street continues to confuse and deceive the public, and position people to fail, and the fiduciary concept is just another one of these lies by omission. That's the problem with our industry today, so many Americans are getting advice from the wrong people and buying into disastrous advice. Don't fall for it.

The point I'm trying to make here is don't get caught up on titles or designations, what you're really looking for is someone who will tell it like it is, and make the same recommendations to you that they'd make to their own mother (and yes, I've sold my mother financial products). In my opinion, this is more important than any title.

That's why when people ask me if I'm a fiduciary, I say, "Absolutely not!"

Telling It Like It Is

Growing up on a lake had a big effect on my imagination as a child, and I had big dreams of being Captain of my own boat. One summer, when I was twelve years old, a certain sport fishing boat on Lake Michigan had caught my eye, and I decided I wanted to be the first mate on it. I was always amazed at how many fish the pros were catching compared to us, and I was determined to figure out how to catch more fish.

My father encouraged this ambition in me, and soon I began writing letters to the charter boat Captain, begging for an opportunity to become a "mate." Shortly after, I received a call from one George C. Bolhouse, the owner and operator of The Bolhouse Charter Service. My family was familiar with Bolhouse, he was a pioneer in Lake Michigan Sport Fishing, and he had a reputation for being a difficult guy to work for. He was known for telling people like it is, and he was a yeller.

> "What I learned from this experience is that the best in the industry aren't going to tell you what you like to hear, they're going to tell you like it is."

Despite his bad reputation, I ended up working for George as his mate for many years, and even went on to become the youngest licensed captain in the United States. I had a thirty year run as a Lake Michigan Charter Boat Captain, and it was all because I took a chance on working with George Bolhouse.

What I learned from this experience is that the best in the industry aren't going to tell you what you like to hear, they're going to tell you like it is. They don't have the time or the patience to come up with elaborate lies, and they may come off as abrasive. I pride myself on the fact that I tell my clients straight up if I think they are going to lose money by taking certain risks. I'm not comfortable putting my client's money into an account that's going to generate fees paid to me every quarter for the rest of their lives. Not being a fiduciary allows me to tell it like it is. But if I'm a fiduciary, I am now legally obligated to share those options with you that I think are horrendous and come up with 'pretty sounding' reasons to convince you why you should follow my advice.

The bottom line is I never want to put your money in a spot where you might lose it. I will not violate the "Mother Standard." I don't want to be looped into the same garbage advice these talking heads are giving, and I don't care if that makes it look like I'm going against the grain, or going up the escalator, while everyone is going down. I guarantee you I'm smart enough to pass a test and get a license and be a fiduciary tomorrow afternoon, but I will never do that unless the government forces me to do so, because I don't believe the advice that fiduciaries are giving the general public is good advice. And I don't need to be a fiduciary to responsibly take care of my clients' assets.

The point I'm trying to make is, don't get hung up on the term fiduciary, it doesn't make much difference. Learn to look outside of the advice Wall Street has to offer. Understand that the masses are easily steered in the wrong direction, so if everyone is turning right, then maybe you should consider turning left.

Now that we've dealt with a major misconception in the market about being a fiduciary, let's talk about real solutions that many of my clients have used with much success. The next chapter is all about fixed index annuities, and I'm going to tell you why I'm the "Pied Piper" for them.

CHAPTER 8

My Safe Money Mission: Annuities

"An account that never loses money, spends no time recovering from losses, and earns a reasonable rate of return will, over time, likely outperform an account that goes up and down with the stock market."

Tom Jacobs

The other night I was giving a lecture at one of my live events. Standing in front of a room of about forty people, I was on a mission to help them understand that the safest place for their money is in annuities — and given the amount of misinformation on the market today, that's not an easy task.

Once I had the group's full attention, I said, "What you are hearing tonight about annuities isn't what your adviser is going to tell you. If you call him tomorrow, you won't hear this from him. In fact, you'll hear the exact opposite!

"He'll say — *Annuities? Why in God's green earth would you do that?* He'll warn you, you're going to get low returns, you'll tie up your money, and you have to commit to a time period, etc.

"What you need to do is ask him, 'Listen, Fred, if I keep my money with you is there any chance I could lose my money? What about fees? Will I keep paying fees for the rest of my life?'

"If he's honest, he'll say there's a chance you could lose money, and yes, there's fees for the rest of your life, then there's your answer on why you're moving your money. If he's dishonest, he'll say anything to deflect you from asking him more about it. And if that happens, you should get your money out of there, and come see me. Chances are, I'll beat him in the long term anyway."

I looked around the room to see if I was getting through to them — a few of the audience members were nodding their heads.

As you can tell, my speaking style is aggressive, straightforward, and very direct. This might scare some people but judging by the reactions I get at our live events, a lot of people find this refreshing.

I asked them, "Why am I at dinner with you tonight, instead of at home with my wife? I don't want to sell you anything: in fact, unlike the last presenter, I don't need any extra clients. I'm on a crusade. I'm on a safe money mission.

"The truth is, I don't have to host eighty-five live dinner events every year in expensive restaurants, run radio spots almost daily, do television appearances, and have my face on fifty billboards around town. My goal isn't to get you to book an appointment. If someone isn't a good fit for my services, I don't waste a single second of their (or my) time. My goal is to expose these concepts to as many people as possible before the next market correction — because markets tank, they always do — and my fear is that most Americans are set up for a major disruption in retirement. I want to prevent that from happening because it's going to be devastating, just as it was for my family."

I finished. "That's why I'm at the most expensive restaurant in Grand Rapids buying dinner for a group of total strangers, instead of at home with my wife Shelly in our beautiful lake house."

> "Folks, I play for Superbowl rings, I play for championships, and I play to win. I want you to win in your retirement. And to do that, you need annuities."

"Folks, I play for Superbowl rings, I play for championships, and I play to win. I want you to win in your retirement. And to do that, you need annuities."

The Pied Piper of Fixed Annuities

My favorite color is orange. A few years back, I went on an 'anything orange' buying binge. One night, I was browsing online, and I found a killer orange Speedo, and immediately purchased it. Unbeknownst to my family, it arrived a week later, and I quietly stashed it in the closet, waiting for the perfect opportunity.

One night I left my family sitting in the hot tub, relaxing, unaware that I was changing into my new orange Speedo. A few minutes later, I strode out of the house with my bright orange (two sizes too small) Speedo. My girls shrieked and my wife became completely unhinged laughing. They still talk about it to this day.

It was worth every penny.

There are two morals to this story: one, fat men shouldn't wear Speedos (especially bright orange ones), and two, you shouldn't be afraid to make people uncomfortable or stand out from the crowd. If you haven't noticed, I'm not afraid to address the elephant in the room. In fact, sometimes I'm the elephant!

So far in this book we've addressed the problems in our financial landscape very clearly and given you enough examples and case studies to support the claims. Now, we're presenting a primary product that will achieve the solutions we're looking for.

I call myself the "Pied Piper of Fixed Annuities." People have already heard all the myths and objections, but they haven't been introduced to the concepts of indexing in terms of the benefits; the protections; the guaranteed income; the reasonable rate of return; and the peace of mind that annuities can give them. In other words, once people fully understand what fixed index annuities can do for them — they'll follow the Pied Piper.

My job is to explain annuities to you in a way that fills in the missing information you need to make the right decision about whether this product would serve you in retirement.

Three Types of Annuities

> "AMERICANS SHOULD CONVERT AT LEAST HALF OF THEIR RETIREMENT SAVINGS INTO AN ANNUITY."
>
> -U.S. Treasury Department

If you open up your browser and type 'annuity' into the Google search bar, you'll get three-million hits — and 2.9 million of them saying don't buy annuities. This is what I like to call "Fake News," or propaganda designed to deceive by omitting the truth.

The annuities that we recommend actually have several major benefits:

1. Your money is not in the stock market

2. Principal protected

3. Zero fees (dependent on fulfilling your contract)

There are three basic types of annuities: fixed annuities that work just like a bank CD, where you get a fixed rate of interest for a specific number of months (i.e. three percent for four years, no more no less); the second type is fixed index annuities which is our specialty, they have no guaranteed rate of return, however they do have a guaranteed floor of zero, meaning we can never lose money when the market tanks, and we gain the upside potential up to our cap; then there's a variable annuity, and these are the most popular annuities in existence today, and because variable annuities are the most popular type, annuities have gotten a very bad name, and that's simply because variable annuities are not principal protected, as I've said before.

If your money is at risk and you're paying annual money management fees — then I agree with those 2.9 million people saying don't buy an annuity! But I also want you to understand that's not what we're talking about here, we're talking about fixed index annuities, which is an insurance product. Your money is not directly invested in the stock market, and many of these types of annuities have absolutely zero money management fees as long as you fulfill the time commitment.

This is what I tell my clients when talking about indexing, I ask them, "What if you could put your money into an account and when the market goes up, you go up — but if the market goes down, you stay the same?

"Let me make sure you understand what I just said. One, what if there was a way to put some money in an account and you would never lose one penny, even when the market goes down. Two, the account has zero fees as long as you fulfill the contract, so they'll never dig into your returns. There may be an income rider that can add fees, but the point is that in general you're not paying annual money management fees every year. And three, what if the account gave you an upfront bonus that was credited on day one — and that's real money that is all yours, that you can immediately start earning interest on. Is that something you would like to know more about?"

Most of the time they say, "Yes, of course!"

Then there are those skeptics that say, "It's too good to be true."

My response to them is, "It's not too good to be true. It's true."

Fixed index annuities have been in Michigan since 1994, and there are thirty-four companies that offer these accounts today — they do exist — but there are a couple of things you need to be aware of. First, you have to commit to a timeframe.

Just like if you bought a five-year CD tomorrow, and two years later, you wanted to take out all the money, you'd be penalized. It's the same concept with a fixed index annuity. Almost any time increment can be purchased, but the best time frame I've found is somewhere between five and ten years. In my opinion, it's the sweet spot, but whatever time increment you choose, with most FIAs you can usually take out ten percent of the account value after the first year without any penalties.

Some people think this is a catch. This isn't a catch and let me tell you why. What we're talking about here is your retirement money. Personally, I've never seen anyone take out their entire retirement nest egg and blow it all in one go. Generally speaking, people spend their retirement money a little bit at a time, as they are using it to supplement their Social Security, pensions, and other investments.

With that said, you still have to leave your money somewhere until you need it. So, these are your options: leave it in the bank, not growing; leave it in your investment accounts and just pray it's still there when you need it; or you could give it to me, and I'm going to put it in a fixed index annuity. I can't tell you how much is going to be there when you need to withdraw it, but I can tell you that even in the absolute worst possible case scenario, you will still have 100 percent of your money.

Annuities are very low risk, but you have to understand how they work. You have to be smart about it.

Being Smart with Fixed Annuities

Retirement money needs to last as long as you do. The challenge is we don't know how long you are going to last.

Fixed index annuities allow you to take out ten percent of what you invested after the first year. For instance, if you bought a fixed index annuity, you dumped some money in, and you waited one year, but then you started withdrawing ten percent per year and you continue to do that every year after that — how long is the money going to last? Well, we don't know exactly because we don't know how much it's going to grow, but what we do know, is if we're taking out ten percent a year, it's certainly not going to last forever, and you're probably going to run out of money. But if that's what you want to do with your money, go for it! You can take out up to ten percent per year, and it's not a catch, it's just something that you need to understand and be aware of.

The point I'm trying to make is, the terms are flexible, but you still need to be smart with your annuity.

The second thing that you need to know is that you're not going to get all of the upside, but you can never lose all your money. There's something called a cap on your fixed indexed annuity. The best way to think about a cap is that there's a limit on how much money you can make. Let's pretend you've bought an annuity and the cap is ten percent, so that's the most you could earn next year, but there's also a floor of zero.

If ten percent is the most you can make, and zero is the worst, and the market goes up to twenty-three percent, what would you get? You'd get ten percent, because that's your cap, but what if the market goes down twenty-three percent? You would be credited zero for that year, but you'd also lose zero money, you'd retain 100 percent of your account value. So, what's more important?

In my opinion, it's much more important to have an account that never loses money. You'll never spend one second recovering from losses, and time is of the essence when it comes to retirement. If you're paying zero fees, and can get reasonable returns over time, that account is going to have the most money in it. I've never had a client fail with this strategy, it happens every single time. Not because we're crushing it with whopper returns every year, but simply because they never lose!

An indexed account is going to give you a better return, without the risks and fees. You're still participating in the power of the market, but you're doing it differently by putting a floor under your feet, so each year your gains are locked in and captured, and you never forfeit them. Even if the next year the market goes down, that's the power of a fixed indexed annuity, it resets annually. There's no other vehicle on planet Earth that would provide that.

That's why I am the Pied Piper of fixed indexed annuities, because I believe with every fiber of my being, that every family needs to have some of their money in a fixed indexed annuity. From my experience, nothing creates peace of mind in retirement like a fixed index annuity. The only thing left to determine is how much of your money needs to go into this type of vehicle.

Now that we've busted the myths surrounding annuities and opened you to new opportunities for securing a fabulous, stress-free retirement — we can introduce you to another revolutionary concept: The IUL, Indexed Universal Life Insurance, and its superior tax free benefits.

CHAPTER 9

IUL Tax Free Benefits

"I BELIEVE IN INDEXING, AND THERE ARE
TWO VEHICLES COMBINED WITH AN INDEXED
CREDITING STRATEGY THAT ARE PRETTY DARN
HARD TO BEAT: 1. INDEXED UNIVERSAL LIFE
INSURANCE, AND 2. FIXED INDEXED ANNUITIES."

Tom Jacobs

In August 2017, Jim Harbaugh, the head coach for University of Michigan Football became one of the highest paid coaches in college football thanks to the deferred compensation package the university put together for him, and a huge part of his package was Index Universal Life Insurance (IUL). Shaquille O'Neal recently purchased several large IUL insurance policies. Walt Disney famously leveraged all of his assets, including his life insurance policy, to bootstrap his theme park after the banks turned him down for a business loan. Today his legacy, the Disney theme parks and movie studio, are world renowned.

There are only two places the government allows us to save and withdraw our money without paying taxes, Roth IRA, and life insurance. In particular, Indexed Universal Life Insurance policies (known as IUL's) allow you to grow your money tax-free over time. The problem is, hardly anyone has heard of an IUL.

When you hear the word life insurance — what do you think of?

Most people's mind immediately goes to the death benefit. Usually, we associate life insurance with our father's or our spouse's policy, something that will only come into play in the event of a tragedy. Well, there's a new breed of life insurance policies that are designed to be of benefit to us while we are alive, not just provide a death benefit.

When properly structured, an IUL gives you a safe place to save and grow your wealth — your gains are locked in and protected against potential losses, including expected losses in the form of taxes. Not only do you have a traditional death benefit of a life insurance policy, but your money is protected from the ups and downs of the stock market, growing tax-free until you are ready to use it. Unlike traditional retirement vehicles, such as 401K's, you can withdraw your money tax-free at any time, at any age, without extra fees.

In my opinion, the tax free income is the biggest benefit to an IUL. Of course, it has some other bells and whistles — I'm typically not buying it for the death benefit or long term health care — but it's exciting to also have those at no additional cost. Starting to save money in an indexed life insurance policy in your twenties, thirties, and forties can save you a lot of hassles along the way, but most people aren't thinking about these things until they're in their late fifties, early sixties, and at that point they've already built the bomb and now we need to diffuse it.

Don't worry, even if you're starting late, there are plenty of ways to move your money into the right place.

Find the Right Basket

Like I said earlier, I'm the Pied Piper of indexing. I believe in indexing, and there are two vehicles combined with an indexed crediting strategy that are pretty darn hard to beat: 1. Indexed Universal Life Insurance, and 2. Fixed Indexed Annuities.

As the "Pied Piper," I often help my clients move their assets from a taxable bucket, to a non-taxable bucket, to defuse their "Tax Time Bomb." Using an indexed annuity as a temporary parking garage and taking advantage of the free withdrawals at ten percent, we can easily transition money out of a client's 401K or IRA and fund an IUL over a period of five to ten years.

The reason we do this is because when you retire, you're going to want to maintain the same standard and quality of life you had while you were working. If all the income you're going to be receiving in retirement is coming from a qualified retirement account, then it is subject to taxes, most likely at whatever tax bracket you were in before you retired. Coupled with the fact that taxes in this country historically go up, not down, we know that we need to be proactive in our savings, and if we've created a tax time bomb, then we need to defuse that immediately.

> "MOST PEOPLE UNDERSTAND THE CONCEPT OF DIVERSIFICATION — DON'T PUT ALL YOUR EGGS IN ONE BASKET — BUT HARDLY ANYONE IS DIVERSIFYING THEIR TAX STRATEGIES."

Most people understand the concept of diversification — don't put all your eggs in one basket — but hardly anyone is diversifying their tax strategies. We spend all this time diversifying our assets, putting them into various retirement accounts, and yet, there's almost zero tax diversification.

Nobody can tell the future, we don't know what will happen with our investments, or how many dollars we will earn — but there is a 100 percent certainty that you will have to pay taxes on those dollars. It's just a matter of when.

I like to tell my clients there is nothing wrong with finding a good basket to put our eggs into, or several baskets. Diversifying is a great way to mitigate some of the risk of losing money. You can minimize your tax risk by using non-taxable buckets like IUL's, and if you can't get insured for health reasons, then use indexed annuities or a Roth IRA.

My question is: if you understand the power of diversification, and you are already diversifying your investments, then why aren't you diversifying your tax risk?

So, why not find the right basket to put your eggs into?

Everybody is Biased

There are several different categories of financial experts on the market, CPA's, Wall Street brokers, Hedge Fund managers — and most financial advisors are biased.

What do I mean by that?

Most advisors are focused on returns, growth, and asset allocation, they aren't addressing taxes or retirement. For instance, the focus of your CPA is saving you money on taxes today, because that's what their clients expect of them. How many CPAs are actually having conversations with their forty and fifty-year-old clients about how much taxes they will pay upon retirement, and how to reduce their taxes when they retire at age sixty-eight or seventy? Almost zero.

The same goes for Wall Street, if you talk to an advisor at a brokerage, they will tell you to invest in mutual funds, stocks, and bonds because their bias is to grow your money, and so their focus is on rate of return. Then, you have your financial market propaganda machine, which are all the talking heads you see on Fox business, and CNBC, the Dave Ramsey and Suzie Orman types. Typically, these people advertise their platforms to you, because they make money when your assets are under their management. So, their bias is to get your money under management. There's no money in tax reduction for Dave Ramsey, so his focus is on eliminating debt; same for Suzie Orman. When they do mention life insurance, it's to tell people never to buy these policies. Of course that's what they'll say because they're biased — there's no money in it for them!

Out of all the types of financial experts I've mentioned, who is out there talking about protecting your retirement from being blitzed by income taxes in ten or fifteen years? Nobody. Therefore, nobody hears about Indexed Universal Life insurance policies.

The information isn't being suppressed, there isn't some giant conspiracy against you, it's simply not the focus of the bias of most financial experts. That's the way the world turns, everyone is self-interested, and we all need to make money — so people will usually talk to you about what is in their best interest.

That being said, you're probably wondering, what is my bias? Well, our focus is on your retirement. I'm the Pied Piper of annuities, that's my bias. We're focused on maximizing your retirement, and to do that we have to minimize your taxes. To date, I haven't found a better way of reducing your tax risk than through indexed life insurance.

These policies can be used for anything — college funding, purchasing real estate, replacing a vehicle —

and you have access to the cash throughout your life, it's not locked away in a 401K with fees and red tape. You don't have to ask permission or fill out a loan application at the bank, it's your account, no questions asked.

When it comes to my clients, I don't care if they put their money into an indexed annuity or an indexed life insurance policy, as long as it's indexed or principal protected, and they're not paying fees. Generally, they're more than happy to give up some of the upside as long as their protection is guaranteed. And if they get a death benefit and long term care benefits, as well as tax free income — it's game on, baby!

So, if life insurance policies are so great, why isn't everyone doing it? They are. Rich people have been using these types of policies for years — Walt Disney, Shaquille O'Neal, Jim Harbaugh, etc. — as a huge part of their overall financial strategy to create guaranteed income for life. So, why should rich people have all the fun? Start creating your own peace of mind in retirement today!

CHAPTER 10

WINNING IN RETIREMENT

"RETIREMENT IS LIKE A LONG VACATION IN VEGAS. THE GOAL IS TO ENJOY IT TO THE FULLEST, BUT NOT SO FULLY THAT YOU RUN OUT OF MONEY!"

Jonathan Clements

S o far in this book, these are the conversations we've had: how to avoid building a "tax time bomb" with your retirement savings, the importance of income planning for peace of mind, and the superior benefits of indexing, annuities, and life insurance policies.

The time to act is now.

Everything you've read so far is either making sense to you (and you have a knot in your stomach), or it's not. If you are starting to feel like this book was written for you, let's get together — I've included some contact information in the back of this book. If not, then not. Like I said, the goal of this book wasn't to get clients in the door. My goal was to get the *right* people to book an appointment with me.

By now you've gotten a sense of my style as an advisor. I've shared my philosophies and personal stories with you, and you know that I always tell you like it is. Now I just have one last thing to tell you...

My parents were robbed of their retirement. Today, they are seventy-eight years old, living in the same condo as before, and they've completely recovered from the correction of 2008. They even have more money today than they did before the meltdown. But in my family's case, it's 100 percent meaningless. It doesn't matter at all, because my dad has a medical condition, and my mom is his caregiver, and they rarely leave the condo. Their quality of life has declined since 2008, and that's a terrible thing to see.

I don't want this to happen to your family. You have to take action today, and the best way to start is by being careful of the advice you are taking on financial matters. Everyone has a bias, and as long as you understand their incentives, you can make an informed decision as to whether or not to listen to them. That being said, it would be my privilege to help your family.

If you do become a client of mine, this is what you can expect:

Every one of my clients gets a three ring binder — not just the clients I like — everyone. Inside, there's a summary of their accounts all on one page. They can easily see where their money was, where it is today, how much is in their account, and whether or not they have any bonuses. At any point, if they need anything that can't be found in this binder, they can stop by or call the office. (I have the best staff on planet Earth; they wake up every day excited to serve our clients.) And if that's not enough, my clients can always call the insurance carrier at any time, and I've included the number. I like to meet with my clients periodically, and I have them bring the binder, so we can review their statements, and see if our plan is doing what we want it to.

I know change is hard and making a major change when it comes to money is ten times harder, but if this is making sense to you, then you have nothing to lose by contacting me. Trust me, I don't want to waste a single second of your time, or mine. Getting your money back after a market correction doesn't buy you anything, if you can't enjoy it. My goal is to help you enjoy your retirement while you can, by creating an exclusive income plan that gives you peace of mind in the fact that you'll never run out of money. I want to help you win in your retirement. And I promise you, all your bases will be covered — a tax strategy, a product suggestion, and a comprehensive strategy to help you "play to win" in retirement.

The only way that happens is if we get together

To schedule your consultation go to

www.retirementdomination.com